It's Easy To Play Beethoven.

Wise Publications
London/New York/Sydney

Exclusive Distributors:
Music Sales Limited
8/9 Frith Street, London, W1V 5TZ, England.
Music Sales Pty. Limited
120 Rothschild Avenue, Rosebery, NSW 2018, Australia.

This book © Copyright 1988 by
Wise Publications
UK ISBN 0.7119.1521.0
Order No. AM 71739

Art direction by Mike Bell
Cover illustration by Paul Leith
Compiled by Peter Evans
Arranged by Daniel Scott

Music Sales' complete catalogue lists thousands of
titles and is free from your local music shop,
or direct from Music Sales Limited.
Please send £1.50 Cheque or Postal Order for postage to
Music Sales Limited, 8/9 Frith Street, London W1V 5TZ.

Printed in England by
Caligraving Limited, Thetford, Norfolk

Allegretto from
Sonata Op.14 No.1

Composed by Ludwig van Beethoven

Bagatelle Op.33 No.6

Composed by Ludwig van Beethoven

Allegretto from Symphony No.7

Composed by Ludwig van Beethoven

Emperor Concerto
First Movement

Composed by Ludwig van Beethoven

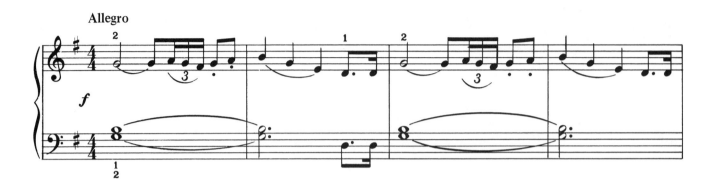

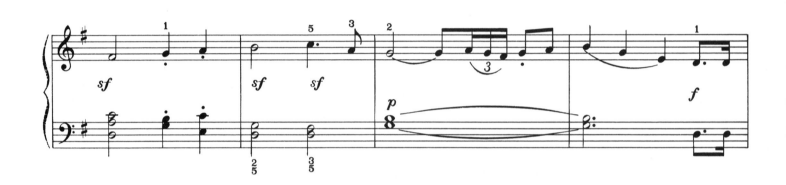

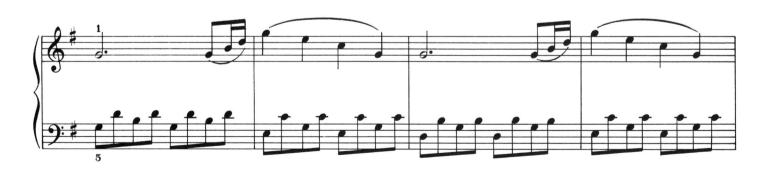

Adagio from Pathétique Sonata

Composed by Ludwig van Beethoven

Canto Pastoral
from Symphony No.6

Composed by Ludwig van Beethoven

March from Egmont Overture

Composed by Ludwig van Beethoven

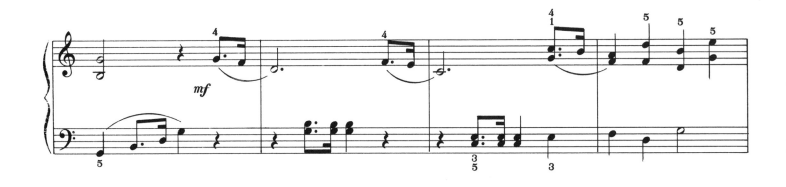

19

Eroica Symphony
(Theme)

Composed by Ludwig van Beethoven

Funeral March

Composed by Ludwig van Beethoven

Für Elise

Composed by Ludwig van Beethoven

Minuet In G

Composed by Ludwig van Beethoven

Romance In F Op.50

Composed by Ludwig van Beethoven

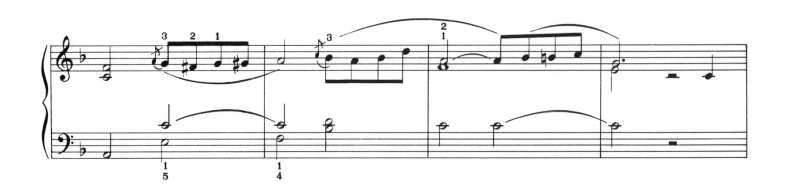

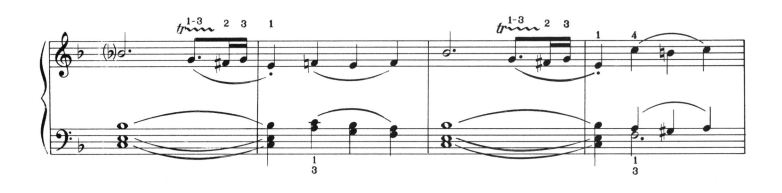

27

Symphony No.5
First Movement

Composed by Ludwig van Beethoven

29

Moonlight Sonata
First Movement

Composed by Ludwig van Beethoven

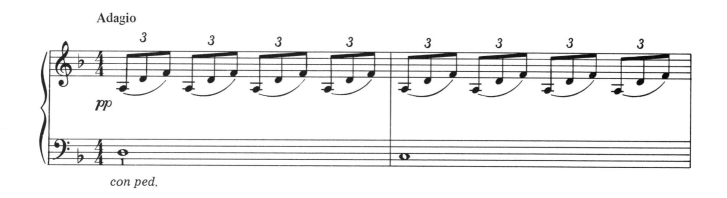

Piano Concerto No. 4
First Movement

Composed by Ludwig van Beethoven

Allegro moderato

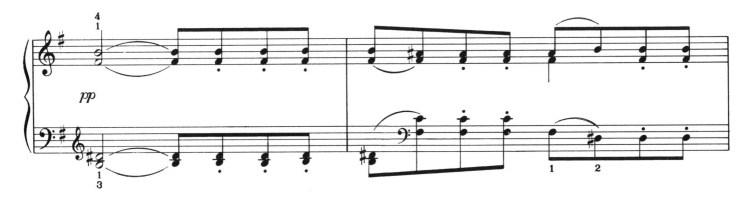

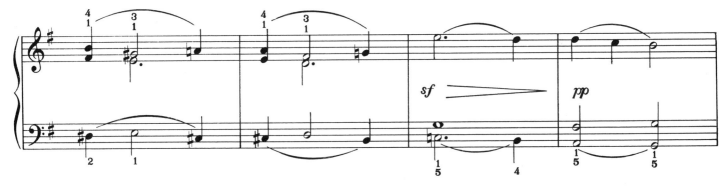

legato

dim.

pp

Minuet from Op.49 No.2

Composed by Ludwig van Beethoven

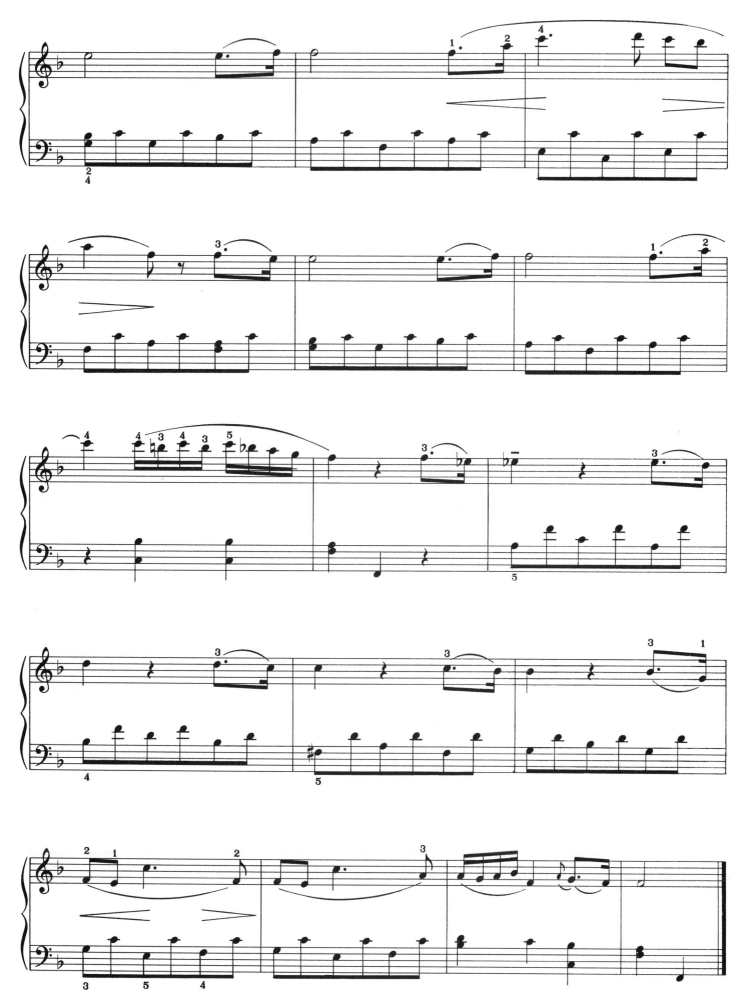

Violin Concerto
First Movement

Composed by Ludwig van Beethoven

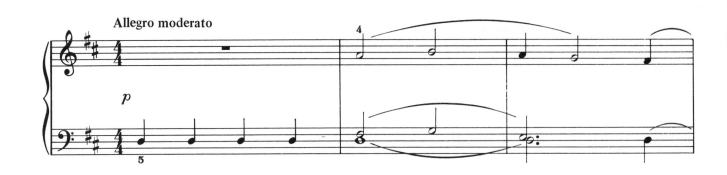

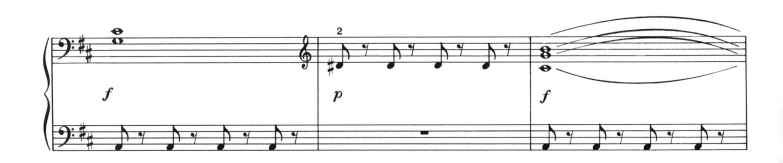

Symphony No.9
Theme from Finale

Composed by Ludwig van Beethoven

Theme From
Variations Op.26

Composed by Ludwig van Beethoven

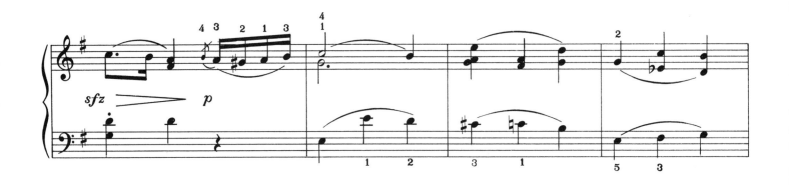

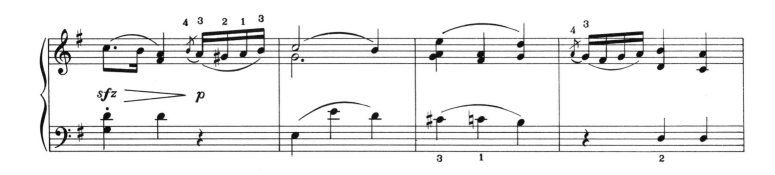

Symphony No.8
First Movement

Composed by Ludwig van Beethoven

4/94 (17683)

The Beatles

Enya

Phil Collins

Van Morrison

Bob Dylan

Sting

Paul Simon

Tracy Chapman

Eric Clapton

Pink Floyd

New Kids On The Block

Bryan Adams

Tina Turner

Elton John

Bee Gees

Whitney Houston

AC/DC

Bringing you the words

All the latest in rock and pop. Plus the brightest and best in West End show scores. Music books for every instrument under the sun. And exciting new teach-yourself ideas like "Let's Play Keyboard" - in cassette/book packs, or on video. Available from all good music shops.

and music

Music Sales' complete catalogue lists thousands of titles and is available free from your local music shop, or direct from Music Sales Limited. Please send a cheque or postal order for £1.50 (for postage) to:

Music Sales Limited
Newmarket Road,
Bury St Edmunds,
Suffolk IP33 3YB

Buddy

Five Guys Named Moe

Les Misérables

West Side Story

Phantom Of The Opera

Show Boat

The Rocky Horror Show

Bringing you the world's best music.